jodi hills

TRISTAN PUBLISHING

Minneapolis

To Darryl...I never fell so hard for spring.

Library of Congress Cataloging-in-Publication Data

Hills, Jodi

  Love / written by Jodi Hills.
     p. cm.
   ISBN 978-0-931674-63-1 (alk. paper)
   1. Love. I. Title.
   BF575.L8H56 2011
   306.7--dc22
                              2011009201

TRISTAN PUBLISHING, INC.
2355 Louisiana Avenue North
Golden Valley, MN 55427

Copyright © 2011, Jodi Hills
ISBN 978-0-931674-63-1
Printed in China
First Printing

I can't remember not loving you.

Yet, you look at me, and it feels as
though we just met.

How do you do that...
live through the colorful and messy
seasons of my heart,
and arrive each day as spring?

You are as constant
and surprising,
as warm,
as hopeful as spring,

and I joyfully live in the
beauty of it all.

It's a beautiful thing, this love,
and I do love you.

I really mean it. Not in the diluted
way as those words are so often
scattered, like "have a nice day,"
not like that.

I love you.

Until I felt it for you, I don't think I knew what it meant. I'm certain I never really heard those words, really heard them, until you said them to me.

It was like, well, it was like
you were speaking to me in our
own language.

You made fresh these words,
sculpted and stroked the same letters,

until they fit perfectly into this
empty space in my heart, and filled it.

I guess that's a lot of responsibility to put on these words of love.
I know they need to be supported.

I'm good with that. Something this
precious deserves that kind of attention,
and you have mine!

You have me...all of me...
I wish that didn't include
my flaws, but it does.

*all
of me*

I know I make mistakes.
I don't believe in movie lines
like "never having to say you're
sorry." I need to say a lot of things.
"I'm sorry,"
"please forgive me,"
and "I'll try to do better."

I want to be the best person I can
be, for you, and for me...for this
world. I want to do better.
I want to be better. You continue
to bring that out in me.

You're such a good person, a loving
person. I just want to be near you...
with you.

It's a crazy thing this love,
to feel someone's heart
beating in your own,
and still not be close enough.

WOW!

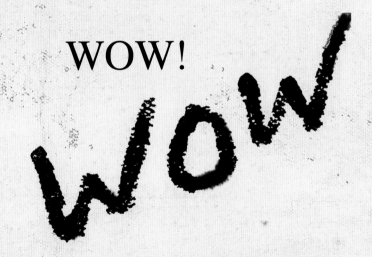

It's fun to love you.
I love to hear you laugh.
I love to feel your smile.

I've seen your eyes sparkle when you look at
me - ME - and I still can hardly believe it.
I guess the thing is, I do believe it. I believe
you love me too. What an honor to share this
love. I'm so proud of it...

                                           of you.

I want everyone to see,

they *have* to see,

it's a BIG LOVE!

I love you. Consider love's repetition
a path. The words are markers on this
journey. I love you. I want to travel
in it, through it...whatever life brings.
And I mean whatever. I love you when
you're happy. To be a part of that joy
is indescribable.

It's OK if you're sad
sometimes. You're not made
of stone and I love that.
I love that you feel things, that
you can be moved to tears.
It makes me trust your smile.
It makes me trust your heart.

Your beautiful heart...I love
that you made room in it,
just for me, and that you
expand it every day.
In your heart,
I am never alone.

I knew it the day we met.
I knew if I could live in
your heart, it would be
amazing.
 It is!
  You are!!!

complete

I love you. Though I love to hear
you say it back, this one is just for
you. It's complete.

I love you.

It's for you…
about you.

I'm in love with YOU!

I love you. Big in meaning, these words are too small to hide behind. What we say and what we do, will always show through. I hope my actions match what you deserve.

You deserve someone
to be nice to you all the
time...to be thoughtful,
caring, tender,
understanding, fun,
joyful and kind.

You deserve to be loved.

you are
someone
to be
loved

I want to love you that way.

Look at you...
you are someone to be loved.

Look at you...
I can't help but love you.

I look at you and I want to tell you
what I remember about our first kiss.

I want to tell you that you are
morningtime.

You are afternoons.

You are rest.

true

I want to touch your face and
tell you that I believe in you.
I want to put your hand to my
heart, so you'll believe all of it
is true.

I want to tell you that
I like you,
that I'm drawn to you,
that I think about the things you say,
that I value your opinion,
and I trust your instincts.

I want to tell you that
you make lunches
special and Tuesdays
holidays. You make real
moments of moments.

I want to tell you that I feel lucky to know
you...so lucky that you know me, that you
know my name, that I'm so grateful to hear
you call it, whisper it.   I want to share
with you how your heart pillows to mine,
and I am home.

I want to tell you that I pray Hemingway
was right, that "there would always be the
spring..."

always

All these feelings rush through
my heart and my veins and my
brain. The words race to my
mouth, but three always win.
I just hope that you can know
them all, feel them all, as I
speak the words, "I" and "love"
and "you."

I love you.